MASTERPIECES IN MINIATURE
TEDDY BEARS

BOOK THREE:
BEAR EPHEMERA

GERRY GREY

APPLE

A QUARTO BOOK

Published by Apple Press
6 Blundell Street
London N7 9BH

ISBN: 1–84092–198–6

QUAR.MTC

This book was conceived, designed and produced by:
Quarto Publishing plc
The Old Brewery 6 Blundell Street
London N7 9BH

Project Editors: Nicola Birtwisle, Joyce Bentley
Senior Art Editor: Penny Cobb
Copy Editor: Sarah Vickery
Designer: Ruth Shane
Photographer: Paul Forrester

Art Director: Moira Clinch
Publisher: Piers Spence

Manufactured in Hong Kong by Regent Publishing Services Ltd.
Printed in China by Leefung-Asco Printers Ltd.
9 8 7 6 5 4 3 2 1

CONTENTS

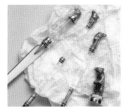

INTRODUCTION

One of the delights of being a teddy bear collector is seeking out bears in the course of your travels. Often, items related to teddy bears will catch the eye: a teddy brooch, a ceramic bear, or pretty bear postcards. This book is for you if, like me, you cannot help but acquire anything remotely connected with bears.

The most precious and valuable of all teddy bear ephemera is sterling silver, particularly if it is hallmarked. Gold pieces are unusual, although contemporary designs on rings or charms are now readily available. Costume jewelry made during the last twenty to thirty years is particularly popular–most collectors love nothing more than to adorn themselves with their favorite teddy bear necklace and head off to a bear fair or shop.

Crystal glass makes a superb medium for stylish bears, and many of the world's most distinguished glassmakers, including Lalique and Baccarat, have produced collectors' editions.

Many of the great porcelain factories of the world have taken teddy bears as their subject. Ceramic manufacturers have also produced many teddy bear figures, although in today's market resin-based materials have almost taken over.

Of all the media employed to depict the teddy bear the printed postcard must be the most prolific. Postcards are extremely popular and easily affordable, although complete sets in pristine condition command high prices.

The range of collectables associated with the teddy bear is so vast that, whatever your taste, you cannot fail to find some form of ephemera that will enhance your collection. Those pieces illustrated in this book merely scratch the surface–there is much more waiting to be discovered.

FAR LEFT: *Engraved lead crystal silhouette by Mats Jonasson.*

LEFT: *Ceramic pins by Boyds Bears.*

ABOVE: *Steiff also produce watches, like these 1998 ones.*

The Essentials of Collecting Teddy Bear Ephemera

What to look for

• Decide which of the many media you find interesting and concentrate on purchasing those in the best possible condition you can find and afford. With glass, silver, or paper, quality is most important to the piece's overall value.

Improving your knowledge

• Read all you can and refer to any specialist books or magazines that cover your chosen medium.

• When dealing with silver, hallmarks and manufacturers' marks help to establish age and maker. Similarly, porcelain marks provide much information about a piece.

• Gather information at fairs that specialize in general antiques, silver, or postcards.

Where to buy

• Antique fairs are likely to prove the most worthwhile hunting grounds, but be careful—unlike most teddy bear specialists, there are antique traders who can be "inventive" when it comes to prices or information about the piece in question. Remember also that porcelain is a material that is frequently copied, so be very careful when looking for the genuine article.

• Teddy bear shops can sometimes be a source of ephemera. Most teddy bear fairs have dealers who display some ephemera.

ABOVE:
"Anne," a limited edition china figurine, was made by Jan Hagara in 1983-1984.

• Auction houses can be a good source, but you will need to concentrate on a particular specialty. Occasionally, you will find teddy bear ephemera at teddy bear auctions, particularly if an entire collection is up for sale.

Caring for ephemera
• Porcelain, glass, silver, and ceramics can be displayed among your favorite bears, but all will need regular cleaning. You should consult the relevant specialist book for advice. Paper ephemera must be kept away from sunlight–items such as postcards will survive in good condition if stored in special collectors' albums with protective covers. Do not, however, put them into an album with sticky backing, as you will render them worthless instantly.

LEFT: *A pair of American teddy bear earrings.*

BELOW: *An attractive group of true-to-life wooden carved bears from the Black Forest region of Germany.*

CERAMIC BEARS

FROM FAMILIAR CHARACTERS LIKE WINNIE THE
POOH TO SOME LITTLE FIREMEN WITH A STORY
TO TELL, HERE ARE THE BEST CERAMIC AND
PORCELAIN MINIATURE BEARS.

Heartland Reunion Bears

HEIGHT: 3 in (7 ½ cm)
COLLECTABILITY FACTOR:
Extremely limited edition, produced
for a world-famous event.

Every five years teddy bear lovers gather at a very special convention in a little town called Clarion in the middle of Iowa. Called the Heartland Reunion, it was the inspiration of world-famous teddy bear artist Steve Schutt and the town's council, with the aim to create greater awareness of the region, which few people would ordinarily visit. In 1995 each conventioneer was presented with a specially designed, limited edition, resin-based bear by America's favorite figurine manufacturer, Boyd's Bears and Friends. This type of special commemorative piece is always highly treasured by those teddy bear lovers who were most fortunate to attend.

Silly
Old
Bear

HEIGHT: 2 ¼ in (5 ¾ cm)
COLLECTABILITY FACTOR:
Very limited availability.

Winnie the Pooh is probably the world's favorite literary bear, with a range of memorabilia to reflect his popularity. The Pooh collector therefore needs to be selective and discerning. Try to seek out unusual Winnie the Pooh items, or pieces that are limited in quantity or by time period. This hand-painted china Winnie the Pooh sculpture was available for purchase over a single open house weekend—June 7 and 8, 1997—at Disney World, Florida. It is part of the Disney Classic Collection series, which depicts original animated film scenes. Here, one of Pooh's most famous poses is recreated, as he attempts to float up the honey tree with the help of his balloon.

Children with Bears Figurines

Height: 6 ¼ in (16 cm)

Collectability factor:
Royal Doulton figurines are
quality English porcelain, limited
production. Jan Hagara figures are
limited edition.

Porcelain and china are excellent
media for creating evocative studies
of times past. The porcelain figurines
here are made by Royal Doulton, one
of Britain's most famous modern
manufacturers, famed for its
enormous range of porcelain
figures. These hand-painted

figurines illustrate the sensitive and subtle childhood poses typical of the Childhood Days range. They are titled "And So To Bed," produced in 1981, and "And One For You," produced in 1982. Jan Hagara's limited editions of china children with teddy bears originate from the United States and have long been favored by collectors everywhere. "Cristina" was made between 1984 and 1985 and has been beautifully sculptured and produced as a limited edition.

Rupert
the Bear

HEIGHT: 3 ¼ in (8 ¼ cm)

COLLECTABILITY FACTOR: Beautifully
interpreted.

Rupert the Bear was created by Express Newspapers in 1920s London as a regular cartoon character drawn by artist Mary Tourtel. She was responsible for the first 10 years of Rupert drawings but was succeeded by Alfred Bestall. It was Alfred who was responsible for the wonderfully illustrated and colorful annuals that commenced in 1936. Rupert is very dear to British hearts, and even today he has an incredible following. Needless to say Rupert is another literary bear who has become highly commercialized. Although he has been reproduced on countless occasions as a figurine, these simple resin characters, designed and produced by the English Lorrie-Mac Company, beautifully portray Rupert's unique appeal. They are hand-molded and painted, and date from 1994.

Limited Edition Teapot

HEIGHT: 3 in (7 ½ cm)
COLLECTABILITY FACTOR:
A limited edition of the world's
favorite bear.

Produced as a functional teapot, this delightful piece of Winnie the Pooh pottery was designed by British designer Paul Cardew. Part of a range of special limited editions called the Disney Character Teapot Collection, this teapot is number 433 of 5,000 and was created exclusively for Disney in 1995. A wonderful array of individual figures brightly adorn this unusual but most attractive teapot. Collectors will find a wide range of interesting teapots available, either styled as teddy bears or simply decorated with teddies or related subjects. They are great fun to collect and will also enhance your china display cabinet.

Blaze

Height: 3 ¼ in (8 ¼ cm)
Collectability factor:
Unique, hand-signed, special
edition of four.

Unfortunate circumstances led to
Blaze's creation. A fire at Peter and
Frances Fagan's house almost
destroyed their beloved collection of
teddy bears. Had it not been for the
timely intervention of the local fire
department, the collection would
certainly have been consumed by fire.
As a special thanks, Peter, who owns
the famous Colour Box ceramics
company, decided to create a
special bear called Blaze to
raise funds for the
Fireman's Society. Bought
at a Colour Box
charity auction in
1997, these three
hand-molded
and painted
bears are part
of an edition of
only four Blaze

bears. One bear is signed by Peter
Fagan, and the other two have the
signatures of all the firemen involved
inscribed on the bears' helmets. The
other bear (No. 1) remains in the
Colour Box museum.

Porcelain Bears

Karin Buckley is a young British artist and designer specializing in the 18th-century British porcelain technique known as Staffordshire pottery. Layer upon layer of color is fired onto the china sculpture, with subject matter usually restricted to historical figures and farm animals. The House of Ashley decided to adopt these traditional techniques to produce two large and three small teddies that make up a range known as the Chelsea Bears. Limited to 2,500 pieces each, Jeremy, Timothy, and Augustus were created in 1994. The designer has shown exceptional skill in recreating the softness of fur and the spirit of a traditional teddy bear using a hard medium such as bone china.

HEIGHT: 4 ¼ in (11 cm)
COLLECTABILITY FACTOR:
Exceptional quality English china.

"Happy" around the World

HEIGHT: 2 ¼ in (5 ¾ cm)
COLLECTABILITY FACTOR:
Special event
commemorative edition.

"Happy" was chosen as a mascot for the renowned Teddies of the World Convention in 1993. It was intended as a symbol of unification for teddy bear enthusiasts, who used their love for bears to raise money for charity. In 1989 "Happy" fetched £55,000 at auction, and the bear's public appearances and support for special events has generated considerable funds for charities benefitting children worldwide. The figurine was sculptured by the very talented Laurie McFaul of the British company Lorrie-Mac, and was made using a resin-based molding technique. "Happy" was hand-cast and painted, and made to a very limited number of 500. Illustrated is the prototype together with No. 1 of the edition.

GLASS *and* ENAMEL *Bears*

DELICATE AND EXQUISITE, GLASS IS AN UNUSUAL BUT EFFECTIVE MEDIUM TO DEPICT BEAR MINIATURES. ALSO, WE SHOWCASE SOME COLORFUL ENAMEL PIECES.

Crystal Glass Bears

Baccarat, one of the world's leading glass manufacturers, was founded in 1766 near Lunéville in France. During the art deco period they were second only to the famous firm of Lalique. Still in existence today, Baccarat is renowned for the sheer quality of its elaborate glass sculptures, produced by some of the world's leading craftsmen with experience passed down through generations of skilled glass makers. These exceptional bears are of purest quality crystal glass and illustrate the classic beauty of aesthetic form, which only the finest crystal glass can provide. Although rather expensive, the breathtaking style of these two tiny teddy bears is a collector's dream.

HEIGHT: 2 ¼ in (5 ¾ cm)
COLLECTABILITY
FACTOR: Finest quality
from a world leader.

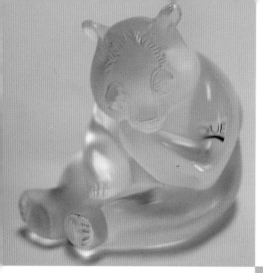

There is no doubt as to the standing of René Lalique as the world's leading glass sculptor. In 1914 he commenced glass production from a workshop in Combs-La-Ville, France and a few years later moved to Alsace. An extremely gifted and

A Special Panda

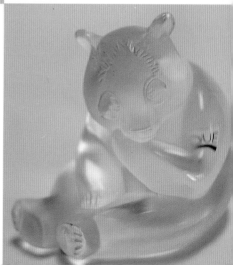

HEIGHT: 3 ½ in (9 cm)
COLLECTABILITY FACTOR:
The world's leading glass
sculptor firm.

sophisticated designer, Lalique
developed his own unique
techniques in sandblasted glass,
acid etching, coloring, and
even molding. Few of Lalique's
designs have ever incorporated
bears, but this delightfully
sensitive portrayal of a
singularly lovely, and sadly
endangered, panda bear, is an
exception.

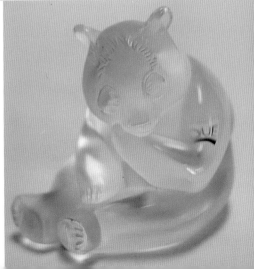

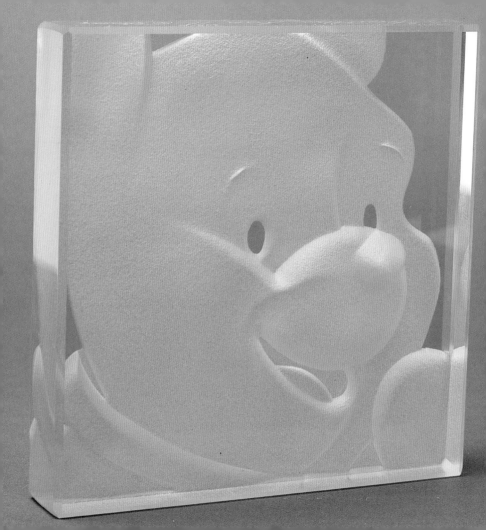

Glass Silhouettes

HEIGHT: 5 in (12 ¾ cm)
COLLECTABILITY FACTOR:
Very limited edition.

Produced for Disney in 1997 as a commissioned design, this distinctive silhouette engraving of Winnie the Pooh is a most desirable collectable. Made from pure blue/green glass, Pooh's profile is made by acid etching into the glass, giving it depth and dimension. Highly sought after, this piece was limited to only 1,000.

18th Century Style English Enamelware

HEIGHT: 2 in (5 cm)
COLLECTABILITY FACTOR:
Quality English craftsmanship.

Tiny trinket or pill pots have been favored by ladies for centuries because they are particularly easy to discreetly conceal. Sometimes rather plain, but usually of intricately engraved silver or finely decorated enamel, these treasures are rarely decorated with subjects relating to teddy bears: until now, that is. During the past decade, Halcyon Days, a leading manufacturer of traditional English enamelware, has extended its repertoire to include teddy bears. The firm employs original 18th-century techniques, and here intricate hand-painted illustrations of colorful teddy bear designs decorate the tiny pots.

WOODEN BEARS

HERE YOU'LL FIND TRADITIONAL GERMAN AND SWISS BEARS MADE OF WOOD, AND THE USE OF A VERY UNUSUAL MATERIAL TO MAKE STYLISH BEAR SCULPTURES.

Black Forest Wooden Bears

The Black Forest and Bavarian regions on the German/Swiss borders have always been famed for their wonderful wooden carvings, especially those based on true-to-life bears. These fine quality wooden bears have always been immensely popular and are considered the best in the world. Always extremely difficult to positively identify and age, these bears date from between 1910 and 1920. Look for sharp, well defined carving and the hard and heavy, but richly colored, brown pine. Beware of the many reproduction bears flooding the marketplace, which lack the quality of the real thing and use an inferior, lightweight material.

HEIGHT: 4 in (10 cm)
COLLECTABILITY
FACTOR: Beautifully
hand-carved.

Black Forest Bears

HEIGHT: 2 ¼ in (5 ¾ cm)
COLLECTABILITY FACTOR:
Unusual designs.

Contrary to their name, these bears are more likely to have originated in Switzerland than Germany. Based on real-life bears, the sheer range of unusual compositions that these delightful wooden pieces can take appears to be unlimited. Usually the carvings are quite large, but here we show two small, intricate pine-wood carvings set on to corks to form wine bottle stoppers. The jolly dancing bear is quite unusual, although some may prefer the sheer strength and well defined carving of the bear's head, which has produced a wonderful character. Both date from 1910 and they would be considered jewels in any collection.

Bears of Black Gold

HEIGHT: Mother bear 4 ¼ in (11 cm)
COLLECTABILITY FACTOR: Unusual medium.

Coal, once called "black gold," must surely be one of the strangest materials ever used to create a decorative bear. Made by Classique, a company based in South Wales, this mother and her two small bear cubs present a harmonious group picture, and show just how effectively coal can be shaped. The technique involves mixing coal dust with resin, and then molding the figure. The definition on these bears is both crisp and neat, and they are quite beautifully made. This group was created in 1992, and is at present fairly inexpensive. However, the unusual medium could easily make this piece a future collectable.

SILVER BEARS

4

MINIATURE BEARS LOOK GREAT
RENDERED IN THIS PRECIOUS METAL, AND,
AS WE SEE HERE, HAVE ADORNED MANY
ATTRACTIVE AND USEFUL PIECES.

Gentleman's Rare Silver Writing Set

There is little doubt that British silversmiths have produced some of the finest silverware in the world. The quality of their workmanship is second to none, and this attractive gentleman's writing set is also testament to their creativeness. The silversmith who made it was John Collard Vicery, who worked from 1899 to 1908 at a studio in London's fashionable Bond Street. Comprising a letter opener, pencil, pen, and personal hand seal and made from hallmarked silver, these true-to-life bears each have tiny ruby eyes set on the finest pure crystal glass stems, with silver mountings to create a truly wondrous writing set. This is an extremely rare set and would probably be impossible to replace.

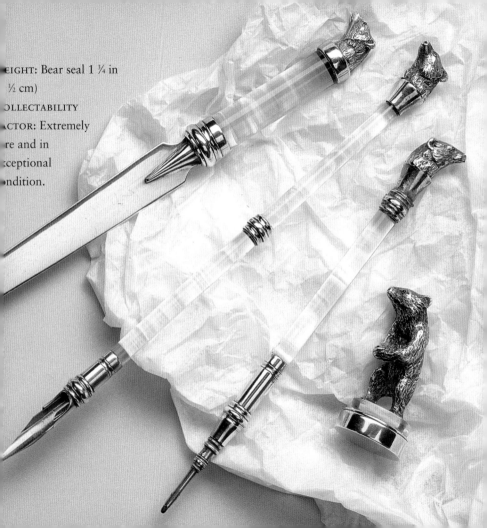

EIGHT: Bear seal 1 ¾ in
½ cm)

OLLECTABILITY
CTOR: Extremely
re and in
ceptional
ndition.

Silver Napkin Ring
and
Toothpick Holder

HEIGHT: 2 ¼ in (5 ¾ cm)
COLLECTABILITY FACTOR:
Very hard to find.

Some of the finest British silverware has been created by the hands of the silversmiths of Birmingham, who were renowned for the variety of their designs. Usually pieces will carry an English silver hallmark, which can be used to accurately date the work. Unfortunately the hallmarks on these particular pieces are rather indistinct and we can therefore only suggest that the napkin ring's style dates it to around 1885, while the toothpick holder dates from around 1890. The napkin ring depicts a standing bear pushing against the ring, on which sits a beautifully styled bumblebee. The toothpick holder, although much simpler in design, remains quite distinctive, with two small bears supporting the silver cup.

Animali
Silver
Bear

HEIGHT: 3 in (7 ½ cm)
COLLECTABILITY FACTOR: Unusual modern design.

It is surprising what you can find in the most unexpected of places. This nice silver teddy bear was discovered in a small, backstreet showroom in London's Mayfair. Part of the Animali range, the designer's concept was role reversal using animals and humans: here we see a modern style of teddy bear nursing a human baby. A really unusual and fun piece, the bear was created by designer F. Scappiticca in his Sheffield Studios in 1997 and is made from hallmarked English silver.

Silver
Ring
Holders

44 SILVER BEARS

HEIGHT: 2 in (5 cm)
COLLECTABILITY FACTOR: Unusual theme
and hard to find.

These sterling silver fashion ring
holders are an unusual concept. The
large, finely detailed bear next to the
ring-holder tree is unmarked, but is
likely to be English and from around
the turn of the 20th century. A far
simpler composition is the tiny silver
bear with ruby eyes surmounting the
central ring holder pole. Although
hallmarked with the distinct maker's
mark A+LL, the maker cannot be
positively identified at this time,
although we know that the piece was
made in Birmingham, England, in
1909. It is always extremely difficult to
find good quality silverware with teddy
or bear designs, so you'll need to be
very diligent if you wish to build up a
good collection.

5 BEAR JEWELRY

FUN TO WEAR AND EASY TO COLLECT, CUTE
TEDDY BEAR JEWELRY LIKE THIS IS HUGELY
POPULAR AMONG BEAR ENTHUSIASTS,
WHO WON'T BE SEEN WITHOUT IT.

Watches and Belt Buckles

VARIOUS SIZES
COLLECTABILITY FACTOR:
Bear watches are a great
favorite among teddy bear
collectors.

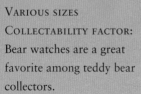

It is easy to make a watch attractive to a teddy bear lover—simply add teddy bears! Here, we have put together a small collection of English bears to prove the point. Some watches bear the familiar names of manufacturers such as Cherished Teddies, Muffy VanderBear, Winnie the Pooh, and of course Steiff. Another practical yet stylish collectable is belt buckles. Ladies' belts tend to utilize contemporary teddy bear designs, and are often elaborately clustered with imitation precious stones, while men must be content with true-to-life bears.

Necklaces, Earrings, and Bracelets

VARIOUS SIZES
COLLECTABILITY FACTOR:
Attractive, sometimes quite
valuable.

These teddy bear necklaces, earrings, and bracelets are all from contemporary manufacturers but are nonetheless extremely attractive. A wealth of designs are available, and while some are traditional, others may be considered rather frivolous. Sometimes made of solid gold or silver—the occasional diamond can even be found—most pieces of jewelry will be made from gold- or silver-plated metals. All are great fun to wear, which is precisely why teddy bear collectors love them.

Teddy Bear Pins

Although teddy bear collecting is a modern phenomenon, it is amazing how rapidly the market has spread across the world. Many collectors travel regularly to special events, shows, and conventions and they are often given mementos, such as these pins, to commemorate their visit. In addition, manufacturers and retailers have discovered the virtue of issuing

small gifts as a "thank you" to regular customers. While pins are currently inexpensive, there is little doubt that this type of memorabilia will eventually become popular with teddy bear collectors, and the cost of purchasing old pins will probably increase. Now is the time to accumulate a collection. Display it on your favorite teddy bear's clothing!

VARIOUS SIZES

Diamonds Are a Girl's Best Friend

Diamonds are a girl's best friend, or so sang Marilyn Monroe. These gems may not be diamonds, but they will certainly provide enough sparkle to brighten up anyone's life. Little evidence exists to confirm whether jewelry designers of yesteryear considered teddy bears as an appropriate subject for jewelry. Perhaps they thought them rather trite and frivolous. Fortunately, modern-day designers have no such inhibitions and there is an abundance of teddy bear brooches on the market today. Some are simple and cheap, while others are much more sophisticated and really quite expensive. Regardless, there is no doubting their charm and appeal to teddy bear lovers, who particularly enjoy wearing them to specialist teddy bear events.

VARIOUS SIZES
COLLECTABILITY FACTOR:
Fun and mostly inexpensive to collect, although some can be expensive.

All KINDS *of* EVERYTHING

FROM LADIES' STOCKINGS TO A VAST SELECTION
OF POSTCARDS, TEDDY BEARS HAVE APPEARED
ON THE MOST DIVERSE AND UNUSUAL ITEMS.

Bear Brand Stockings

HEIGHT: 4 ¼ in (11 cm)
COLLECTABILITY FACTOR:
Hard to find.

The enormous popularity of teddy bears has made them an excellent choice for advertising manufacturers' products. Probably the best known of these in Britain would be the Chad Valley Co. Ltd. teddy bear, which became known as the Bear Brand Stocking Bear. These stockings were first made during the 1920s and a lovely Chad Valley bear was chosen as their mascot. This rather delicate bear is printed onto cardboard and has feet that revolve around to create the impression that it is walking. Dating from 1935, it is just one example of Bear Brand printed ephemera that you can collect.

Teddy B and Teddy G Tipping Trays

HEIGHT: 4 ¾ in (12 cm)
COLLECTABILITY FACTOR:
Unusual—depicts early
bear history.

Seymour Eaton was the creator of a series of stories about two bears collectively referred to as the Roosevelt Bears, but individually called Teddy B and Teddy G. First published in 1906, during Theodore Roosevelt's presidency, the books became great favorites with the American public. By 1908 the bears were frequently being used to adorn tip trays to collect gratuities from satisfied customers. Made from pressed steel, the decoration on these varied across the country as they always advertised local companies. These trays illustrate the Worcester Salt Co. of New York.

Postcards have long presented a cheap but acceptable method of communication, a tradition that persists even in these days of high technology. Just about every conceivable theme has been portrayed on a postcard, and it is fortunate for us that postcard manufacturers at the turn of the 20th century were quick to realize the potential appeal of teddy bear postcards— there is an abundance of them available today. It is quite easy to date postcards accurately, as they will often be stamped or have the date franked on them. Some postcards even carry personal messages, making them even more interesting. The period from 1906 to 1910 is considered the heyday for teddy bears, and is the best period from which to collect postcards, though they can be an expensive purchase.

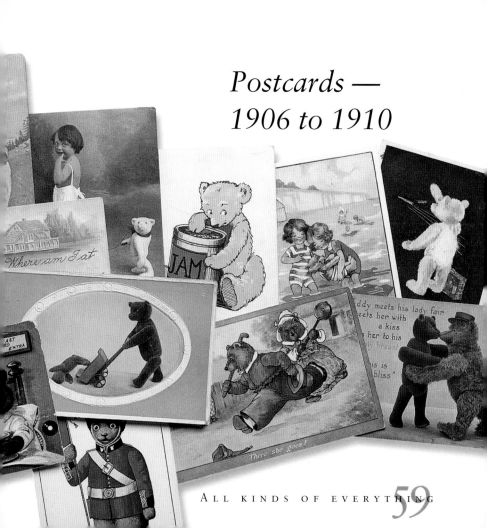

Postcards —
1906 to 1910

Where am I at

JAM

ddy meets his lady fair
eets her with
a kiss
s her to his
dy breast

his is
bliss"

There she goes!

After the postman has knocked at your door
And this little postcard you see
You'll know that who'ever forgets you to-day
That you are remembered by me.

Postcards — 1911 to 1919

Postcards can be found just about everywhere—antique fairs, thrift sales—but hardly ever at bear collectors' events. Specialist postcard fairs are probably the most reliable source, where reputable dealers can always be found with good stocks of postcards to choose from. One must expect to pay a little more for cards at these events, but look out for the more unusual ones. Here a mixture of ordinary and rare postcards from the period 1911 to 1919 is shown. Usually cards were issued as a series of 4 to 6, so look out for cards to make up your set. These delicate pieces of ephemera can command high prices, so one must be careful to store one's collection correctly. Most importantly, keep your postcards out of harmful sunlight, and, if possible, store them in albums that are easy to keep clean and view.

MARGARET TEMPEST

Postcards — 1920 to 1940

An essential consideration for any collector is the condition of the item on offer, and postcards are no exception. Unless it is a card you especially want, you should always look for a quality postcard without any damage. Here we illustrate an unusual array of cards from the 1920s and 1940s. With good luck you should have many happy hours scouring antique shops and collectors fairs to establish and, hopefully, improve your collection.

Index

Credits

The author and publishers would like to thank the following who allowed some of their treasured collections to be included: Rosemary and Paul Volpp, Joan and Mike Woessner, Audrey Poulton, Penny Cobb and my daughter Jenny Waite who typed all the original texts.

Dedication
To my daughters Debbie and Jenny for putting up with me for so long, and, I trust, for a bit longer.

MASTERPIECES IN MINIATURE
TEDDY BEARS

BOOK ONE:
ANTIQUE BEARS

GERRY GREY

APPLE

A QUARTO BOOK

Copyright © 1999 Quarto Publishing plc

Published by Apple Press
6 Blundell Street
London N7 9BH

ISBN: 1–84092–198–6

QUAR.MTC

This book was conceived, designed and produced by:
Quarto Publishing plc
The Old Brewery 6 Blundell Street
London N7 9BH

Project Editors: Nicola Birtwisle, Joyce Bentley
Senior Art Editor: Penny Cobb
Copy Editor: Sarah Vickery
Designer: Ruth Shane
Photographer: Paul Forrester

Art Director: Moira Clinch
Publisher: Piers Spence

Manufactured in Hong Kong by Regent Publishing Services Ltd.
Printed in China by Leefung-Asco Printers Ltd.
9 8 7 6 5 4 3 2 1

CONTENTS

INTRODUCTION

Most people are aware of the enormous worldwide interest in teddy bears, and many have grown up in the company of their favorite teddy. However, there also exists a very special and unique genre of bears that we define as miniature teddy bears. Of course, they cannot be hugged in the same way as larger teddies, but there is no doubting the appeal of these diminutive and charming creatures. They can be found nestled in a lady's handbag, displayed on a lapel brooch, or even secreted inside a gentleman's pocket.

The earliest known miniature bear was made in Germany around 1905 by the world-famous company Steiff, just a few years after the manufacture of their first toy bears. Sadly, few other manufacturers followed their lead. There was, however, another German company called Schreyer and Co—more commonly referred to as Schuco—which set the world of miniature bear manufacturing on fire. During the Roaring Twenties Schuco quickly realized the potential fashion appeal of a tiny bear that would fit into a young lady's handbag. The collection was named "Piccolo" and featured a variety of brightly colored bears created as casings for lipstick holders, compact sets, and perfume. These ingenious creations are highly prized today and are perhaps the most sought-after miniature bears.

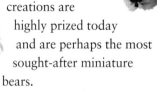

Miniature teddy bears are very much in demand by the modern collector. This book illustrates why these distinctive bears have captured the hearts of teddy bear lovers. It is not a definitive guide but a broad approach to the many wonderful little bears that can be found.

FAR LEFT:
One of the earliest Steiff miniature bears, from around 1905.

ABOVE AND LEFT: *The Schuco Piccolo range of perfume bottle bears was a great favorite in the 1920s.*

The Essentials of Collecting Antique Miniature Bears

What to look for

- Concentrate on age, character, and appeal.
- Small bears have usually been well cared for and are better preserved than their larger cousins. Always purchase the best possible quality and condition you can afford.
- Avoid bears that are badly damaged, unless you relish the prospect of embarking on a difficult restoration.

Improving your knowledge

- Read all you can about teddy bears and manufacturers, and accumulate a working knowledge of styles, construction methods, labels, buttons, and markings.
- If you are lucky enough to live near one of the world's few teddy bear museums, be sure to visit.
- Look out for specialist sales at the large auction houses, where you can see the bears close up and study the catalogue. Going to provincial auctions is not advised—you may know more about bears than they do.
- Join a teddy bear collectors club—there are lots of these around the world. You will find people with similar interests with whom you can exchange useful information.

ABOVE: *Two charming bears from the 1950s and 1960s. The white bear is by Berg of Austria and the fawn one is a Steiff Biegeglieder bear.*

Where to buy

Many teddy bear shops offer a wide range of bears and friendly advice is usually at hand. The best are those where the owner has a good reputation and you do not feel under any sales pressure to buy.

• Teddy bear fairs offer a wide variety of bears and traders in one location.

• Auctions are excellent sources for more unusual and highly collectable pieces. But do not believe everything you are told in the catalogue—you must study the bear for yourself and make your own judgment.

Caring for your bears

• Keep your bears clean by blowing away any airborne dust that accumulates with a camera "puffer" cleaner. This cleaner also has a soft brush that can be used to get deep into the mohair without damaging the backing. Old bears are delicate—do not use a hard brush as this will damage the fabric.

• Store bears at a constant temperature and away from direct sunlight. An enclosed display cabinet is ideal, but be careful of those with lighting, as some discharge lighting emits high levels of ultraviolet, which can bleach the color out of mohair and fabrics.

• Make sure your bears are properly covered on your homeowner's insurance.

• Protect bears from moths and other pests by using whole cloves, cedar wood blocks, or cinnamon sticks sprinkled around the bears or placed in small pots nearby.

BELOW: *These contemporary bears by Steiff prove the company's popularity throughout the 20th century.*

CLASSIC TEDDY BEARS

MINIATURES FROM THE GLORIOUS EARLY

DAYS OF THE TEDDY BEAR: FROM ONE OF

"TEDDY'S BEARS" TO A COMFORTING

FRIEND FROM WORLD WAR I.

A Bear With no Name

HEIGHT: 3 in (7 ½ cm)
COLLECTABILITY FACTOR:
This wonderful, expressive
persona is quite rare.

Without a doubt the most coveted bears among collectors are the large, early bears from the formative era in Steiff's unique history. This famous German company continually produced a wide range of bears, many of which still exist to this day in superb condition. They are a testament to the firm's creative design skills and quality manufacturing capabilities. The small Steiff bears were usually reserved for small children, and regardless of condition they are exceptional little characters. No matter how many you see or own, each is always distinct. This fully articulated bear was made in 1908 and is

made of mohair with small, round glass eyes. It is said that Steiff employed a person who was responsible for making sure no two bears looked quite the same when they left the factory. This would explain the wonderful variety of bears that we find today.

CLASSIC TEDDY BEARS

Roosevelt Campaign Lapel Bear

HEIGHT: 3 in (7 ½ cm)
COLLECTABILITY FACTOR:
Roosevelt memorabilia is highly
prized and this is quite rare.

The association between Theodore Roosevelt, one of America's most famous presidents, and the teddy bear is legendary. The President was quick to realize the vote-winning potential of the link, and when he stood for re-election in 1904 his supporters were given commemorative campaign badge pins depicting, among other motifs, bears. Always a great favorite, this particular piece of memorabilia by an unknown American manufacturer was one of the first occasions that a fur bear was used in connection with Roosevelt. This bear dates from 1904 and was constructed primitively from metal wire on an armature, covered with ribbon and long-pile chenille. It is a delicate piece and quite susceptible to damage, particularly on the paper paws and sealing wax nose, therefore it is unusual to find one in this condition.

Teardrop

The records are unclear as to when the German firm of Steiff made their first miniature bear, but most experts estimate that production began between 1905 and 1906. One of Steiff's early bears, this one has some unusual clues to its age. The button in its ear has the long underscored "F" that limits the bear to a period between 1905 and 1910. It also has sewn bead eyes, used only on very small Steiff animals from the late 1890s to 1905. Teardrop is a fully articulated bear, made of mohair. It is characterized by the slim body with featureless arms, long, well-shaped legs, and large ears set high on the head. These features help pinpoint the bear's age to around 1905. The bear's pretty face has a rather sad, appealing look due to the shiny eyes giving the impression of teardrops.

HEIGHT: 3 in (7 ½ cm)
COLLECTABILITY FACTOR:
Scarce, particularly with
these tiny bead eyes.

Goldie

HEIGHT: 6 in (15cm)
COLLECTABILITY FACTOR:
Very appealing character.

The character of an old bear is hard to define, because it involves many other factors besides the original manufacturing process. The wear, tear, love, and abuse by the bear's owner fashion a unique persona that attracts modern collectors, and Goldie, an early Steiff bear, is a perfect example of this. Although only part of the original nose remains, probably through constant kissing by its original child owner, and the head is now dislodged slightly to one side, this bear still possesses an almost unique persona. Most collectors would certainly love it to be a part of their collection. It is fully articulated and made of mohair, but it is the glass amber eyes that date Goldie to around 1910.

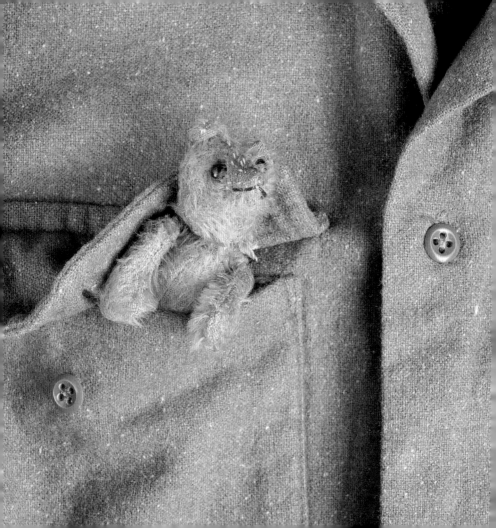

World War I Mascot Bear

When at war, away from their loved ones, men often carried with them a little memento that could be secretly hidden on their person. This is how this little bear, with its strange, long, extended limbs, became a mascot bear for British soldiers in the trenches during World War I. Hidden under their tunics and away from the critical eye of the Company Sergeant Major, these tiny bears were a constant companion and a reminder of the loved ones at home. Made between 1914 and 1918, this little bear is by an unknown British manufacturer and has a one-piece body with fixed joints. Sadly so many soldiers lost their lives, and with them the bears, that they are particularly hard to find today.

HEIGHT: 4 in (10 cm)
COLLECTABILITY FACTOR:
Very difficult to find.

BEARS *of the* 1920s *and* 1930s

AS THE TEDDY BEAR'S POPULARITY GREW, MINIATURE BEARS TOOK ON NEW AND IMAGINATIVE FORMS. HERE WE SHOW SOME OF THE BEST AND MOST COLLECTABLE.

Brownie

The mohair on this splendid Steiff bear, made in the 1920s, is a beautiful, rich shade of brown. Ordinarily brown is a color that most collectors avoid, regarded as dull and unattractive in contrast with some of the brighter and paler colors available, but in this case it is a particularly pleasant shade. The rich brown works well with the bear's rough and rugged appearance, which is exaggerated by one of its amber glass eyes receding well into the eye socket. The long mohair gives this bear a disheveled look and clearly it has been in the wars. A rather surprising find on a bear so small is the side-activated squeaker contained in its fully articulated body. This makes Brownie even more unusual, and without doubt a bear that collectors will crave.

HEIGHT: 5 in (12 ¾ cm)
COLLECTABILITY FACTOR:
Not a popular color, therefore
few would have been made.

White Bear "Roly Poly"

HEIGHT: 3 in (7 ½ cm)
COLLECTABILITY FACTOR:
Rare colour and
size.

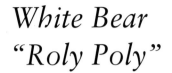

This is in fact
not a Roly-
Poly bear but,
being a rather
mischievous creature, it often
rolls over regardless of how it is
set down—hence the name. It is
an example of a rare 1920s small,
white, Steiff teddy bear and is a
highly prized collectable. A particularly
noticeable trait of the bears from this
genre are the large ears set high on a

well-featured head. Over the years the ears became less prominent and by the early 1950s they were set lower on a much rounder head. This bear is fully articulated and made of off-white mohair. The 1920s witnessed many ups and downs in Steiff's fortunes as they struggled to recover from a devastating recession that followed the 1914–18 European War. This necessitated a drastic change in Steiff's new design concepts and by around 1926 they had recovered their position as the world's leading teddy bear manufacturer.

The Piccolo Compact Bear

HEIGHT: 3 in (7 ½ cm)
COLLECTABILITY FACTOR:
A must for any collector, even
though the gold mohair bear is
quite common.

If ever there was a teddy bear that was a dedicated follower of fashion, then it's this German Schuco bear, part of what became the Piccolo range. The 1920s trend was for stylish, liberated ladies to wear the kind of clothing that was not suited to large cumbersome handbags. Therefore, this novel Schuco concept of a compact bear, which opens up to reveal lipstick, powder, and a mirror, fulfilled the essential fashion prerequisite of the day. It was chic and could easily be concealed within a very small handbag. This bear would date from 1927 or 1928 and is fully articulated, with mohair covering a metal body. Schreyer and Co., or Schuco as the company is best known, virtually ensured the lasting appeal of the miniature teddy bear with its wonderful, innovative design of the Piccolo range of bears.

Compact Bear "Flame"

HEIGHT: 3 in (7 ½ cm)

COLLECTABILITY FACTOR:
This striking color is very appealing and hard to find.

This delicate little Schuco bear has obviously been well used, but retains a good, vibrant body of crimson red mohair and has cut crystal eyes. This vivid red gives "Flame" a distinctive quality, but you can often find these bears in a wide range of unusual colors. The head pulls off to allow the body to open, revealing a tiny powder

compact. Sadly this bear no
longer has its lipstick, although
judging from its pristine
condition it may never have been
fitted. The patent for the compact
bear was applied for in 1927, and
this fully articulated bear would
date from the late 1920s.
Overall condition is always an
essential consideration for
teddy bear collectors,
although sometimes even
more important is the
bear's disposition and
demeanor.

Mohair-Covered Wooden Bears

HEIGHT: 2 ¾ in (7 cm), 2 ¼ in
(5 ¾ cm), 2 in (5 cm)
COLLECTABILITY FACTOR:
Unusual wooden-based bears.

Equally unusual as metal-bodied
Schuco bears are these carved wooden
bears, which are covered over by
mohair. In the traditional style of true-
to-life bears, this range of seated bears
is almost certainly of German origin
and would date from around the
1930s. Conventional glass amber-
colored eyes have been used, and two
of the bears also have glass bead noses
while the other has an embroidered
nose. A purist collector might not
consider purchasing these bears,
but they are attractive and
appealing enough to become part
of any prized collection. They
would also be quite difficult to
procure in today's market.

Atomizer Bear

The Atomizer Bear has to be one of the strangest-ever teddy bear creations. Rather more like a Humpty Dumpty than a teddy

bear, an Atomizer Bear comprises a flat round receptacle, which is filled with perfume through a small screw base. By squeezing the body, a gentle spray of your favorite perfume is forced through a tube that squirts out of the bear's nose. This bear was made around 1930, and has a fixed

head and stubby arms and feet attached to a rotund body. Although this type of bear has never been positively attributed to Schuco it seems probable that no one other than the inimitable Heinrich Muller would have had the imagination and ingenuity to produce such a frivolous but charming little bear.

HEIGHT: 3 ¼ in (8 ¼ cm)
COLLECTABILITY FACTOR: Extremely rare and most unusual.

Perfume
Bottle

HEIGHT: 5 in (12 ½ cm)
COLLECTABILITY FACTOR: Extremely popular
with Schuco devotees.

Heinrich Muller was the founding partner of Schreyer and Co., and it was his imagination and invention that led to the hugely successful Piccolo range of bears. A great favorite with fashionable ladies was this perfume bottle, which the creative Muller originally applied for a patent in 1925, to be made in two discreet sizes, 3 in (7 ½ cm) and 5 in (12 ½ cm). Gold mohair was the most commonly used color, but perfume bottles can be found in many different colors—lavender is possibly the most delectable. There is no doubting the quality of this superb gold-colored mohair bear, made around 1930 and fully articulated.

Metal-
Bodied
Bears

The hard metal body, head, and limbs of Schuco miniature bears easily distinguishes them from other manufacturers' work. Constructed almost like a suit of armor, which is then covered by mohair, this unique concept was patented by Schreyer and Co. and became extremely popular in its day. This particular group of bears illustrates the range available from the mid-1920s through to the 1930s, and indicates the variety of colors and characters that can be found. The early Schuco bears from the 1920s had felt feet and hands, but this was changed to sewn-over hands and feet in the 1930s, presumably because the felt versions soon became detached. These bears' eyes were usually made from black metal studs.

HEIGHT: 3 in (7 ½ cm)
COLLECTABILITY FACTOR:
A variety of different colors to enhance any collection. The early bears with felt feet and hands are harder to find.

A NEW ERA

NEW MASS-MANUFACTURING TECHNIQUES

HELPED TO CREATE A HUGE VARIETY

AND NUMBER OF MINIATURE BEARS.

HERE ARE SOME OF THE BEST.

Post-War Appeal

HEIGHT: 2 ¾ in (7 cm),
4 in (10 cm)
COLLECTABILITY FACTOR:
Becoming increasingly
hard to find.

The Schuco company continued production until the mid-1970s. However, their heyday had definitely been during the 1920s and 1930s. Schuco's post-war production recommenced around 1949 and they made many new bears, including several based on the earlier Piccolo range. The new bear was marketed as the "Original Schuco Talisman" range. It is often quite difficult to distinguish the pre-war from the latter ranges, although recent bears do not quite have the distinctive qualities of their pre-war cousins. However, the early 1950s bears are still much in demand and make a positive contribution to any collection. Shown here is the metal-bodied Panda bear and an early version of the Berlin bear, both of which were made until the 1970s.

Rub-A-Tub-Tub

HEIGHT: 2 in (5 cm), 4 in (10 cm)
COLLECTABILITY
FACTOR: Overall the
group has a lot of
appeal.

Sometimes even the most serious collector will simply take a fancy to a teddy bear that may be of indiscernible manufacture but simply has that "take me home" look. This particular group of cheerful little bears was found several years ago by their new American owners in Australia. As they could not bear to separate them, they were all purchased. Probably of Japanese origin, and dating from the 1950s, they are of primitive construction although fully articulated. They all now live quite happily in a tin bath. There is always room in any collection for bears that may not be in the best condition but have their own special character.

Teddy Baby

In 1930 Steiff created a new range of bears, generically known as the Teddy Baby, which is still in production today. They produced a new version of the range in 1949. However, it was based on early designs, was not popular, and has since become very scarce and decidedly more sought-after than its predecessor. Our 1950 Teddy Baby was sold to its new owner as a 1930s version, presumably because the dealer thought it to be more valuable—how wrong they were. Fully articulated and mohair covered, this wonderful little chap is in good condition.

HEIGHT: 3 in (7 ½ cm)
COLLECTABILITY FACTOR:
More collectable than earlier, original versions.

Original Teddy Bears

HEIGHT: 4 in (10 cm)
COLLECTABILITY FACTOR: Should become
more sought after as we enter the new
millennium.

During the 1950s, in the face of
worldwide competition, the Steiff
Company was forced to produce a
wide range of new designs. Prominent
among them was the Original range,
which included a miniature bear. Being
relatively inexpensive, it could compete
with the cheap bears that were
produced in Japan. It was available in
four colors—caramel, dark brown,
white, and the most popular, gold.
Simple in construction, and of rather
limited character, these 1950s bears
are now becoming sought after. Be on
the lookout for the dark brown bear,
as this one will be the most difficult of
all the colors to find.

Old
or
New?

HEIGHT: 4 in (10 cm)

COLLECTABILITY FACTOR: Currently low cost and easy to find. Possibly one for the future?

The modern collector can often be dismissive of bears from the 1960s and 1970s, but should consider that bears from this period could be nearing forty years of age. There are particular bears from this era that collectors should be looking for now while they are still reasonably easy to find and, of course, affordable. The Steiff Biegeglieder has fixed but bendable limbs and was first made in 1966. The other, caramel-colored bear is also from the mid-1960s and was part of the immensely popular Original range.

MODERN REPRODUCTIONS

4

ANTIQUE BEAR DESIGNS HAVE STOOD
THE TEST OF TIME. THESE EXQUISITE BEARS
ARE AS CAREFULLY MADE AS THE
ORIGINALS, AND LOOK WONDERFUL.

A Celebration of Bears

HEIGHT: 2 in (5 cm)
COLLECTABILITY FACTOR:
Possibly bears for the future.

In recognition of the growing interest in miniatures, the famous Steiff company has produced a XS Original range of their most popular bears from past decades. Intended to be a range of only 12, these tiny bears are fully articulated and covered with mohair. Illustrated here are just a few of those available in 1998, including: Blonde 1930; White 1909; Brown 1951; White 1921; Teddy Baby 1930; and Fawn 1951. These delightful little bears with their lovely little faces represent a welcome addition to any modern collection.

More Modern Miniatures

HEIGHT: 6 in (15 cm), 4 in (10 cm)
COLLECTABILITY FACTOR: Possible future collectables, particularly limited editions.

In addition to the major manufacturers of miniature bears, such as Steiff and Schuco, there have also been a number of quite well-known traditional teddy bear manufacturers who have produced delightful miniature bears. Included here are a selection of standard range and limited edition teddy bears manufactured during the past decade by Gebrüder Hermann and Clemens, two other well-known German manufacturers. All are fully articulated and covered with mohair. Each has its own unique style so these lovely bears should offer plenty of scope to expand your collections.

Modern Replica Snap-Apart Bear

The fortunes of Steiff were revived when, in 1980, they commenced manufacture of limited edition replicas based on original designs from their archives. Replica miniature bears are rarely produced, which is surprising when you consider how many were made in the past. This Snap-Apart bear, originally designed in 1908, was made in 1989. The bear's most interesting feature is that the arms, legs, and head are attached to the body with press-on studs, and therefore can be pulled off. This ingenious bear also has a squeaker concealed in his body.

HEIGHT: 6 ¾ in (17 cm)
COLLECTABILITY FACTOR:
Limited edition of 5,000 worldwide.

Wig Wag
Mechanical
Bears

HEIGHT: 6 in (15 cm)
COLLECTABILITY FACTOR: Unusual, lots of fun, and still quite easy to obtain.

Like many German manufacturers, Steiff have traditionally manufactured bears on wheels, as well as all manner of other mechanical devices. A wonderful illustration of this tradition are these two small, fully articulated bears seated at either end of a metal seesaw. They frantically bob up and down as the seesaw is pulled along. Originally made in 1924, this design was replicated in 1988 in a limited edition of 4,000 worldwide.

Replica Jackie Bear

HEIGHT: 6 ¾ in (17 cm)

COLLECTABILITY FACTOR: Can still be found relatively easily and at low cost. Issued as a limited edition of 12,000 worldwide.

When first introduced in 1953, the Jackie bear represented a completely new design concept for the Steiff company. The rotund features of this bear will be thought rather modern by many collectors, but they were in fact the forerunner of the new breed of teddy bear. Excelsior-filled and covered with mohair, this appealing bear is fully articulated and dates from 1989. Jackie, Steiff reference 0190/17, has a charming expression and remains a particular favorite of those who desire Steiff replicas.

A Trio of Delights

Throughout its history Steiff has always been an innovative company. In recent years it has chosen to produce completely new designs as limited editions, rather than to replicate old designs. The 4 in (10 cm) golden brown, fully articulated bear in a red Father Christmas boot was produced in 1997. The slightly larger 4 ¾ in (12 cm) Christmas Tree bear, with a mohair body and of one-piece fixed construction, was produced the following year. Both editions were limited to 5,000 worldwide and intended to appeal to the modern Steiff collector. The Steiff collectors club has become extremely popular worldwide and in 1997, as a loyalty gift, every new member was given this 2 ¾ in (7 cm) fully articulated replica of an original 1922 miniature bear.

HEIGHT: 4 ¾ in (12 cm), 4 in (10 cm), 2 ¾ in (7 cm)

COLLECTABILITY FACTOR: Unusual and small limited edition, available to club members only, therefore limited numbers.

All Bears are Special

When you gaze into all these little faces
you begin to realize how individual
they all are. It is this individuality that
appeals to the tastes of the collector.
Since their introduction in the 1950s,
Steiff's Original range of bears have
been extremely popular, and during
the 1990s many more designs were
introduced. Of these, those designs
based on bears from an earlier era have
proved the most popular. This
selection includes the 1926 Happy
bear, 1930 Dicky Bear, 1908 Red Bear,
1908 Blue Bear, 1931 Teddy Baby,
1904 Mr. Cinnamon bear, and finally
the 1926 Teddy Clown. These are all
fully articulated and covered with
mohair.

HEIGHT: 6 in (15 cm)
COLLECTABILITY FACTOR:
Bears for the future or to
start off your collection.

TREASURED BEARS

SOME BEARS BECOME SPECIAL FRIENDS FOR LIFE. THESE WELL-LOVED AND ADORABLE LITTLE CHARACTERS SHOW THE SPECIAL BOND BETWEEN PEOPLE AND BEARS.

Winnie the Pooh

HEIGHT: 6 in (15 cm)
COLLECTABILITY FACTOR: Limited number of 500.

Canterbury Bears, a small English company of bear makers, was founded in 1981 by John and Maude Blackburn. The company produces a wide range of teddy bears, although rarely in miniature. However, the Blackburns often produce special editions, such as this limited edition of 500 Winnie the Pooh bears. It was available for purchase only at the 1996 Disney Teddy Bear and Doll Convention, and will therefore be quite hard to find. The bear is fully articulated and soft-filled. The characterization Canterbury has created is based on the hugely popular Disney adaptation of A. A. Milne's original character.

The Magic Personal Touch

HEIGHT: 4 in (10 cm), 2 in (5 cm)
COLLECTABILITY FACTOR:
Personalized to satisfy the owner.

It is not always the manufacturer's creativity which appeals to collectors, but the personal touches that owners often add to their bears. Quite ordinary bears of no particular value can be transformed into amazing little creatures by the addition of a simple garment, particularly if it has been specially made for the bear. This is the case with these crudely made bears from the 1930s and 1950s, by an unknown manufacturer. The introduction of some toy or personal childhood keepsake can also make a positive contribution to the esthetic quality of the bears.

Collective Qualities

HEIGHT: 3 in (7 ½ cm)
COLLECTABILITY FACTOR: Brightly colored bears can be interesting additions to any collection.

The 1950s proved to be an excellent time for Japanese toy manufacturers, as their trade with the rest of the world skyrocketed. Teddy bears were a popular export, and miniatures were made in vast numbers to meet demand. These bears are of primitive construction, although fully articulated, and are not at all distinctive, with only basic, featureless shapes. In fact, they might be considered rather bland were it not for the ravages of time and play that has transformed these little brightly colored mohair bears into cute little characters. They look especially appealing grouped together.

Index

Credits

The authors and
publishers would
sincerely like to
thank the following
for their help and
assistance in
providing some of
their wonderful old
bears for this book:
Rosemary and Paul
Volpp, Jo and Roger
Greeno, and Dean
Howard.

Dedications
With love to my wife
Margaret for her
patience over the
past 35 years and for
enjoying with me the
beary good things in
life.

MASTERPIECES IN MINIATURE
TEDDY BEARS

BOOK TWO:
ARTISTS' BEARS

GERRY GREY

APPLE

A QUARTO BOOK

Published by Apple Press
6 Blundell Street
London N7 9BH

ISBN: 1–84092–198–6

QUAR.MTC

This book was conceived, designed and produced by:
Quarto Publishing plc
The Old Brewery 6 Blundell Street
London N7 9BH

Project Editors: Nicola Birtwisle, Joyce Bentley
Senior Art Editor: Penny Cobb
Copy Editor: Sarah Vickery
Designer: Ruth Shane
Photographer: Paul Forrester

Art Director: Moira Clinch
Publisher: Piers Spence

Manufactured in Hong Kong by Regent Publishing Services Ltd.
Printed in China by Leefung-Asco Printers Ltd.
9 8 7 6 5 4 3 2 1

CONTENTS

INTRODUCTION

What makes a teddy bear artist distinct from a teddy bear maker? An artists' bear is best defined as a bear exclusively designed and handmade by one person—a particularly creative person creating fresh new ideas that are not overtly influenced by the work of others. Artists' bears must have a distinctive aesthetic style, quality, and character that will instantly identify them as the work of one single person.

Teddy bear artistry as a major genre began in the United States in the late 1970s, but did not gain strength and recognition until the mid-1980s. It was not until nearly a decade later that this influence spread to other parts of the world in a serious way.

Even in the early days, the American miniaturists showed an unusual and refreshing creativity, challenging recognized conventions surrounding the concept of the teddy bear.

Gradually, tiny teddy bears appeared in every style and theme imaginable. Then in the early 1990s, foreign artists, particularly those from Britain, began challenging the domination of the Americans, and the ubiquitous miniature artist teddy bear at last took its place at teddy bear fairs and conventions the world over.

In my capacity as founder and principal judge of the British Teddy Bear Awards, sponsored and organized by the British teddy bear magazine *Teddy Bear Times*, I have over the years seen some phenomenal entries in the miniature bears category. I have to admit to an absolute passion for the work of the miniature teddy bear artist, which I hope this book, containing some of my personal favorites, will illustrate. However, this must not be considered a comprehensive "who's who" guide–there are many other excellent artists working in miniature who we have been unable to include.

FAR LEFT ABOVE: *"Baby Bear and Buddy," by Sara Phillips.*

FAR LEFT: *"Masquerade," a limited edition by Kathryn Riley.*

ABOVE: *"Mermaid Bear" by Deborah Canham.*

The Essentials of Collecting Artists' Bears

What to look for
- Originality and individuality that communicate the unique style of the artist
  - Character
  - Quality workmanship and materials
  - Special editions, preferably one-of-a-kind or specially commissioned bears

Improving your knowledge
- Read all you can. The best magazines for artists' bears are the *Teddy Bear Review* (USA) and *Teddy Bear Times* (UK and worldwide), which show the work of both established artists and up-and-coming bear makers.
- Visit teddy bear fairs, shows, and conventions, where you will always be able to find miniature bears and may have the opportunity to speak with the artist as well.
- Most museum collections feature only older teddy bears, with the exception of the Teddy Bear Museum of Naples, Florida and some new Japanese museums.
- Visit teddy bear shops that specialize in artists' bears.

Where to buy
- Teddy bear fairs are probably the best venues because you get to meet the artist. You can sometimes also commission the artist to make a special piece for you—a one-of-a-kind exclusively made for the collector.

ABOVE: *"The Cherry Picker" by Sally Lambert shows the attention to detail that distinguishes excellent from ordinary.*

• Some of the larger teddy bear conventions frequently hold auctions for which artists make special pieces. However, these bears can command astronomically and unrealistically high prices.

Many teddy bear shops sell the works of leading artists and often have their own shop specials. This may be the only opportunity to purchase the work of your favorite artist, as most of the artists in this book are frequently in such demand that their output of bears is likely to be limited.

Caring for your bears

• Keep your bears clean by blowing away any airborne dust that accumulates with a camera "puffer" cleaner. This cleaner also has a soft brush that can be used to get deep into the mohair without damaging the backing.

• Store bears at a constant temperature and away from direct sunlight. An enclosed display cabinet is ideal, but be careful of those with lighting, as some discharge lighting emits high levels of ultraviolet, which can bleach the color out of mohair and fabrics.

• Make sure your bears are properly covered on your homeowner's insurance.

• Protect bears from moths and other pests by using whole cloves, cedar wood blocks, or cinnamon sticks sprinkled around the bears or in small pots nearby.

BELOW:
Barbara Conley's "Holly the Woodland Sprite".

1

BEARS *at* PLAY

TEDDY BEARS GETTING UP TO FUN, GAMES, AND MISCHIEF OF ALL KINDS, BEAUTIFULLY DEPICTED IN MINIATURE.

HEIGHT: 5 in (12 ¾ cm)
COLLECTABILITY FACTOR:
Larger bears normally
produced by these artists.
Limited edition of five.

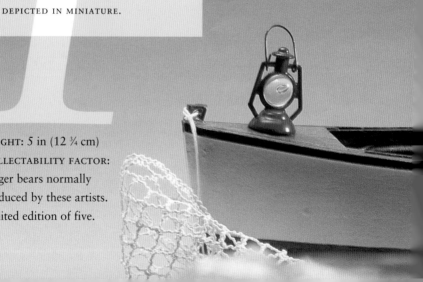

Many men cherish the opportunity to get away and go fishing alone. Our intrepid Fisherbear by Sue and Randall Foskey is fully articulated and made of mohair. He has managed to steal away for a few quiet hours of relaxation in his boat, waiting to land plenty of fish. The Foskeys, whose repertoire comprises such a wide range of award-winning bears, usually produce bears of the larger variety, but they switch to making miniature bears if they feel in need of a change. This provides added appeal to the serious collector.

Old Friends

HEIGHT: 3 in (7 ½ cm)
COLLECTABILITY FACTOR:
Limited annual output.
Real character
bears.

There are few artists who can recreate the personalities of the early bears by Steiff. Barbara Conley is one of the very best, whether she is producing large bears or, as we see here, two miniature bears. Perfect features are essential, but so is conveying the soul of the bear, which we can sense particularly well in the red bear with its wonderful onyx glass eyes. Equally attractive is the multi-colored Panda Clown with a drum. Both bears are made from hand-dyed upholstery velvet, are fully articulated and soft-filled. Conley's yearly teddy bear output is very limited due to her other talent, oil and watercolor painting, making her beautiful bears rather hard to find and a valuable contribution to any collection.

Gerry
at Play

HEIGHT: 4 in (10 cm)

COLLECTABILITY FACTOR: Unique one-of-a-kind bear especially created for its owner.

The highlight of any collection is a bear that has been specially made for you, but it is an honor when your name is associated with it as well. Gerry was made and presented to me by Dutch artist Jane Humme in 1993. The bear has even managed to spell my name correctly with his tiny toy bricks. Based on a traditional Steiff, the charming little bear has been perfectly recreated using old-style mohair, and is fully articulated. It is this type of one-of-a-kind creation that offers the collector something rather special, personal, and unique.

Playboy

HEIGHT: 6 in (15 cm)
COLLECTABILITY FACTOR:
A special one-of-a-kind bear.

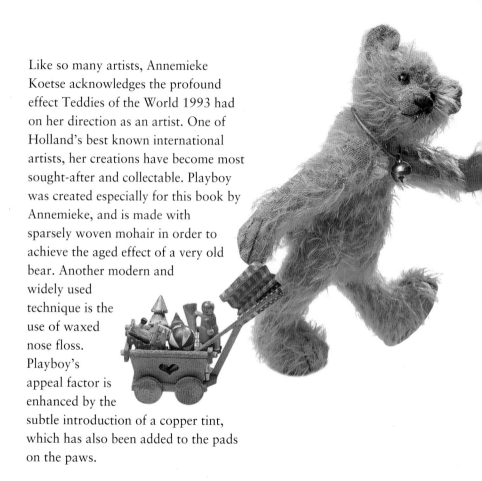

Like so many artists, Annemieke Koetse acknowledges the profound effect Teddies of the World 1993 had on her direction as an artist. One of Holland's best known international artists, her creations have become most sought-after and collectable. Playboy was created especially for this book by Annemieke, and is made with sparsely woven mohair in order to achieve the aged effect of a very old bear. Another modern and widely used technique is the use of waxed nose floss. Playboy's appeal factor is enhanced by the subtle introduction of a copper tint, which has also been added to the pads on the paws.

BEARS at HOME

ADORABLE TEDDIES ENJOYING THEIR
HOME COMFORTS, CAPTURED BY
THE FINEST BEAR ARTISTS.

Tea for Two

HEIGHT:
2 in (5 cm)
COLLECTABILITY
FACTOR: Specialty
piece.

When you have been making bears for as long as Lisa Lloyd there
are few subjects you have not tried to recreate. It is important for
any artist to try to make their work distinct and instantly recognizable,
and Lloyd is most accomplished at this. These fully articulated teapot
bears are made of upholstery velvet and are perhaps one of her more
unusual but interesting ideas. They offer the collector another theme
to pursue and collect. The teapot has been cut away to reveal an
interior in which two small bears are to be found convivially sitting
around the table at teatime. Even the cat seems surprised to see us!

Christmas Rose

HEIGHT: 3 in (7 ½ cm)
COLLECTABILITY FACTOR:
Unique one-of-a-kind creation.

This Christmas Rose was the imaginative creation of top British miniaturist Nicola Perkins. The bright red leather case, an old antique traveling clock case, has been relined with satin surrounded by red roses to create the perfect love haven for our little bear. The bear is made from hand-dyed, old gold-colored upholstery fabric and has a unique chain-link head joint allowing the head to move easily into any position. A slightly sad but perfectly detailed face gives our bear a rather dejected appearance as if she is waiting patiently for her beloved suitor to call and bring back the smile to her face.

Judy
and
Viv

HEIGHT: 2 ½ in (6 ½ cm)
COLLECTABILITY FACTOR:
Unique one-of-a-kind
composition.

It is necessary to explain the
significance of Judy and Viv and how
an actual event led to the creation of
these exquisite and charming bears. In
1993 a group of top American artists
accompanied us on a tour around
Britain and, just for fun, Judy Thomas
had dressed up as the "typical" British
landlady to welcome us to Stratford-
upon-Avon. Viv Vardy-Smith, a most

vivacious serving wench, had
served these Americans beer
at a nearby inn. Billee
Henderson, who sadly
passed away recently, chose
to portray these characters in
the guise of miniature bears. She
has brilliantly captured the essence of
Judy, complete with hairnet, baggy
stockings, and cigarette hanging out of
her mouth, while Viv has gorgeous,
long red hair, and a large bosom. Both
bears were made from upholstery
velvet and are fully articulated with
shaped bodies.

Mother and Baby

HEIGHT: Mother 6 in (15 cm),
baby 2 in (6 cm)
COLLECTABILITY FACTOR: One of a kind.
Major award winner.

"Grandma" Lynn Lumley chose the English Rose motif to personalize her delightful bears. She produced this lovely mother and baby creation, which became the class winner at the American 1992 Toby Awards. The mother bear is made from short pile, off-white alpaca, costumed with *broderie anglaise* dress, including undergarments, copiously decorated with ribbons and bows and Lumley's own unique, hand-made pink roses. The tiny baby is made of plush, with gorgeous, minute, pink pearl eyes and a handsome lace collar.

Mouse Bear

HEIGHT: 2 ¼ in (5 ¾ cm)

COLLECTABILITY FACTOR: Unusual subject, superbly made.

Of all the bear makers it is perhaps the miniaturists who have the greatest opportunity to experiment with new ideas, despite the limited size of the medium. An excellent example of how the standard bear can be expanded upon is illustrated by British artist Carolyn Willis's diminutive Mouse Bear. Clearly it has all the facial characteristics of a bear, yet it also has large, mouse-like ears. The illusion is further enhanced by the introduction of a long mouse tail and tiny furry slippers. This impressive bear is fully articulated and has been expertly created using upholstery velvet.

BEARS
on DUTY

EVERY BEAR HAS A VOCATION IN LIFE, WHETHER
IT BE GUARDING THE NATION OR SELLING TINY
TREASURES. HERE, ALSO, WE SEE A DEPICTION
OF THE INCIDENT THAT STARTED IT ALL.

Old
Scottish
Soldier

HEIGHT: 3 ½ in (9 cm) tall
COLLECTABILITY FACTOR: A
one-of-a-kind piece from a
young artist producing
exciting work.

Style is something very personal and distinguishes the work of any one artist from his or her contemporaries. It must be distinctive, and the work of up-and-coming young British artist Elizabeth Leggat contains these essential ingredients. The Old Scottish Soldier, whose rifle has long since been replaced by a flag, displays the obvious pride that all old soldiers possess. The definitive antique style and features, together with hand-made garments, contribute to the overall dignity of the composition. The bear is made from mohair and felt, and is fully articulated and soft-filled.

Peddler Bear

HEIGHT: 2 ½ in (6 ½ cm)
COLLECTABILITY FACTOR:
One of a kind.

Thematic teddy bears have always been popular, and the Peddler Bear is common among these, because it offers the artist plenty of scope for his or her interpretation. With larger bears it's very easy to find a variety of accessories already made to scale, but imagine how difficult this is when the bear is only 2 ½ in (6 ½ cm) high. With a bear this tiny, everything simply has to be hand-created and it is this attention to detail which makes Louise Peers's creations so highly collectable. The fully clothed construction bear is created using a special type of upholstery velvet that is particularly suited to the numerous minute body parts which go to make up a miniature bear.

DRAWING
THE LINE
IN MISSISSIPPI

Drawing
the Line in
Mississippi

HEIGHT: 2 ½ in (6 ½ cm)
COLLECTABILITY FACTOR:
One of a kind.

The incident in November 1902, when President Roosevelt refused to shoot a bear cub after a poor day's hunting, is well known to all teddy bear collectors. Whether or not Roosevelt's name was actually used to subsequently immortalize the teddy bear is a matter of conjecture. Regardless, April Whitcomb Gustafson has beautifully captured the tension of this historic moment with her portrayal of the rather stout and rugged President and the frightened little cub tethered to a tree. This composition was created in 1988 from upholstery fabric, and the figures are fully articulated. "Drawing the Line in Mississippi" was the famous headline that appeared in the *New York Herald* on November 13, 1902, immortalized as a cartoon character by the renowned Clifford Berryman.

4

TRADITIONAL BEARS

IMAGINE THE PERFECT TEDDY BEAR—CUTE AND CUDDLY, A BRIGHTLY COLORED RIBBON AROUND ITS NECK. HERE ARE SOME BEAUTIFUL MINIATURE VERSIONS.

Mini Murphy

HEIGHT: 4 in (10 cm)
COLLECTABILITY FACTOR: Only around twelve made.

American maker Rosalie Frischman made her first bears in 1983 for her daughters. She found it so much fun that she started creating bears for collectors and attending bear fairs. Her bears have been avidly sought after ever since. Early in her career Rosalie noticed how a shy child lays its head to one side, and she has successfully incorporated this endearing trait into many of her teddy bears. In 1993 this absolutely enchanting, fully articulated little bear, christened Mini Murphy, was added to the range. Only a mere handful were ever made by this most imaginative designer, making Mini Murphy very desirable.

Needles
and
Pins

We all encounter experiences when, for a moment, we become completely consumed with despair because whatever we are attempting to do just is not working. "What do I do next?" seems to be the question this fully articulated bear is asking as he tries to extricate himself from the entanglement of threads. It seems inconceivable that anyone should get so strung up over a few needles and pins. However, his bemused expression has helped American maker Corla Cubillas create a stunning little fellow whom collectors will find irresistible. It is an unusual concept from one of the world's top teddy bear artists, who can successfully make everything from large to tiny bears. Cubillas used long mohair to create this simple little bear in 1989.

HEIGHT: 4 in (10 cm)
COLLECTABILITY FACTOR:
One of a kind.

A Funny Boy

This unusual bear is highly collectable and a classic design.

Considering that this bear was made in 1988, its remarkable design concept has been hard to surpass and has proved to be years ahead of its time. This wonderful character, which in its day set new standards of style and discipline, is the distinctive creation of American artists Howard and Karen Calvin.

Made from upholstery fabric, the bear has an articulated body and fixed head. It absolutely oozes appeal and requires nothing more than a simple ribbon necktie to complete, apart from a small amount of facial rouge. Bears of this genre are very hard to find, but are highly sought-after.

HEIGHT: 3 ⅝ in (9 cm)
COLLECTABILITY FACTOR: Simple but appealing, one of a kind.

Tiny

HEIGHT: 1 in (2 ½ cm)
COLLECTABILITY FACTOR: Small, but with real character and quality.

Many people claim to have made the smallest bear in the world but, to be perfectly honest, a great many of these bears are merely shapes vaguely resembling a bear. To truly claim this, the bear must at the very least display the normal features of a teddy bear with arms and legs that move and, most importantly, realistic facial characteristics. Sandy

Williams's bear is only 1 in (2 ½ cm) in height, and without a doubt is one of the friendliest faces you are likely to find. It even has very small cup-shaped ears and foot pads, is fully articulated, and was hand-sewn in 1988 using ultrasuede. To a collector this smallest bear is just as endearing as the largest, though obviously not quite as cuddly.

Lipstick Bear

HEIGHT: 3 ½ in (9 cm)
COLLECTABILITY FACTOR: Few
of this type of bear exist.

In the 1920s the Piccolo range of miniature bears by Schuco created many novelties, but none as popular as the lipstick or compact bear. It is no surprise, therefore, to find modern artists wishing to recreate the concept, and Sara Phillips has aptly done this with her interpretation called Lipstick Bear. Substantially more elaborate than the earlier versions, made from antique mohair and beautifully dressed in antique and vintage textiles and artifacts, this Lipstick Bear holds its own teddy bear-shaped muff and mirror. The shoes are removable to reveal the lipstick concealed inside. The bear is built around the glass tube. Phillips is renowned for the quality of her unusual and highly collectable miniature bears.

5 COMPANION BEARS

FRIENDS FOR LIFE: MINIATURE TEDDY BEARS
CAN BE VERY AFFECTIONATE CREATURES. HERE
ARE SOME OF THE BEST AND MOST LOVABLE.

*Masoe
and
Mitsuko*

HEIGHT: 2 ¼ in (5 ¾ cm)
COLLECTABILITY FACTOR:
Special design with
traditional costuming.

These marvelous bears are wonderful examples of the finest craftsmanship, created for this book by Japanese mother and daughter, Mari and Akemi Koto. There is a distinctive precision to the traditional Japanese costumes that simply has no equal. Masoe, the boy bear, is made from white fabric and dressed neatly but traditionally in a child's formal silk kimono, dark blue hakama, and greeting fan. Mitsuko, the girl bear, is also dressed in a formal but decoratively embroidered kimono, obi (a belt), ribbon, and greeting fan. Both bears were made in 1998 from upholstery velvet.

Mungo and Titch

HEIGHT: Monkey 4 in (10 cm),
bear 2 ½ in (6 ½ cm)
COLLECTABILITY FACTOR: One of
a kind. Unusual combination.

Throughout the century the teddy bear has been portrayed with all manner of creatures and friends. Monkeys have always had their own band of devotees, so what better than to have these two much loved characters, created for this book by British artist Paula Strethill-Smith, together. Mungo, our monkey friend, has a sorrowful expression, and is clutching Titch the tiny bear with his never-ending arms and legs. It is the clever use of the monkey's wraparound feature that vividly illustrates the closeness of friends which most collectors will find irresistible. The use of antique mohair and felt with a rather worn appearance greatly enhances the attraction to the collector. Both characters are fully articulated, while the monkey has jointed wrists and ankles.

Perfume Bear

For years the work of American Joan Woessner has been coveted by collectors throughout the world, but very few have one of Joan's prized miniatures in their collection. This Perfume Bear is based on the style of bear originated by the German manufacturer Schuco. A larger-than-average miniature bear, it is soft-filled and fully articulated with all the charm of its predecessor, although unmistakably created by modern hands. The use of sparsely woven off-white distressed mohair, felt pads, and long claws on the feet and hand paws emphasize old traits. Decorated simply but delicately with old ribbons, beads, and lace, the bear has its own antique scent bottle.

HEIGHT: 6 in (15 cm)
COLLECTABILITY FACTOR:
Very hard to find.

Two
Cherished
Little
Bears

Many new collectors will look at a magazine or book for guidance as to whose bears to buy. Frequently these only show the top artists, tending to overlook many other bear makers whose work may be equally exciting. Here are just two examples of creations by some lesser known British bear artists whose work is appreciated as part of my collection of miniature bears. Brenda Brightmore, a well known soft doll artist, occasionally produces bears like Thomas, a friendly and lively character, clutching his favorite soft bunny and comfort blanket as he goes off to bed. Amelia, with her favorite doll, all dressed up in her Sunday best and out for an afternoon stroll, is typical of the pleasant miniature bears made by Elizabeth Marsden.

HEIGHT: Thomas 4 in (10 cm)
Amelia 2 ½ in (6 ½ cm)
COLLECTABILITY FACTOR:
Thomas is a real fun character;
Amelia is delicate but a nice
bear for the future.

FANTASY BEARS

WILD AND WONDERFUL FLIGHTS OF FANCY
FROM LEADING BEAR MAKERS: THE ONLY LIMITS
ARE THOSE OF THE ARTIST'S IMAGINATION.

Excalibur

HEIGHT: 4 ½ in (11 ½ cm)
COLLECTABILITY FACTOR:
Commissioned work.
Exceptional quality.

Excalibur was commissioned by me from Kathryn Riley, one of the world's finest miniaturists. This is a mythical subject that continues to stimulate the imagination, and the sheer power and energy of the legend is illustrated perfectly by the exceptional style that Riley has produced. The bear's body armor is hand-made from papier mâché painted silver and gold, and then applied to the finished bear. The long, flowing satin cape provides the finishing touch. King Arthur's proud but determined appearance befits one of the most romantic characters of English history. It is an exceptional example of the finest artistic qualities possessed by only a few special artists.

Chubby

HEIGHT: 1 ¾ in (4 ½ cm)
when seated
COLLECTABILITY FACTOR: A
nice creation from a long-
established artist.

The United States has long been a breeding ground for superlative teddy bear artists. Beth Diane Hogan has emerged as a creative force quite distinct from those miniaturists making more conventional teddy bears. In her childhood she made soft animals from felt, gradually progressing to sculptured clay bears, and finally to the wonderful bears she now produces. Chubby, designed to be seated, is just one of the extensive range of unusual bears that Hogan has produced over the years. This cheeky little bear has a rabbit headband and tiny hand puppet bear. Made from the finest quality, salmon-pink upholstery material and ultrasuede, Chubby and his puppet have simulated jet-black, seed bead eyes.

Patching up Time

HEIGHT: Elf 3 in (7 ½ cm), firefly catcher 2 ½ in (6 ½ cm)
COLLECTABILITY FACTOR: One-of-a-kind special creation.

Comfortably astride his favorite toadstool, warmed by the gentle rays of the early morning sun, the Elf Bear casually sews the finest lace from the web gossamer fibers created by the spider below. Meanwhile an inquiring firefly catcher, returning from a long night's work in the forest, stops to ask the time of day. This harmonious and tranquil group was designed by British artist Sally Lambert, who specializes in unusual and complex miniature creations. The bears are made from a mixture of hand-colored velveteens, while the soft-filled mushroom is constructed from upholstery fabric and embroidered with tiny bees and ladybugs.

Back to Nature

HEIGHT: 3 ¼ in (8 ¼ cm)
COLLECTABILITY
FACTOR: One-of-a-kind
vignette.

Many miniaturists prefer to make several bears and fit them into a setting or vignette, and this is British artist Kay Street's particular area of expertise. The inquiring look on the faces of both fairy bears suggests that we may have interrupted their private courtship activities. The off-white lady bear has a beautiful dress made from a wild orchid, while her male suitor, who is dressed in a garland of wild leaves, has a small bouquet of wild flowers to offer his intended sweetheart. Both bears are fully articulated and made of upholstery fabric. It is the completeness of this composition, which was created in 1998, that will make it a delightful addition to any collection.

Jester

HEIGHT: 6 in (15 cm)
COLLECTABILITY
FACTOR: Special
limited edition.

If it's a quirky, unusual bear you are looking for, then look no further than one made by the hands of Brenda Dewey. There are only a few artists whose bears always convey the sense of whimsy and fun that we can see in this rather wacky Jester. Made as a limited edition of 25 for the Disney World Convention in 1996, this bear has all the distinctive qualities that one would expect from Dewey, who prefers to dye her own fabric and often recycles fashion accessories. It is pellet-filled to improve its posture, and made from upholstery fabric.

Jester
Fairy
Clive

In the Middle Ages the jester was the equivalent of the modern-day comedian. Today,

jesters are an established favorite of teddy bear artists, but rarely do you see the amalgam of historical and mythical elements that we find with Hiro Takahashi's distinctive Jester Fairy, named Clive in dedication to his English friend Clive Thomas. This tiny, winged bear is made

from materials including mohair and upholstery velvet. It is fully articulated, and exquisitely decorated with garlands of tiny roses. Takahashi's work is much in demand throughout the world, and he is one of the few male artists with the ability and dexterity to be able to produce such fine miniatures.

HEIGHT: 4 in (10 cm)
COLLECTABILITY FACTOR:
Unusual subject. One of a kind.

Fantasy Fun

HEIGHT: Fairy bears 2 ½ in (6 ½ cm), Mother bear 4 in (10 cm), Baby bear 1 ¼ in (3 ¼ cm)
COLLECTABILITY FACTOR: Elaborate one-of-a-kind group.

Japanese artist Michi Takahashi made the first of her successful range of exquisite fairy bears in the 1980s. Here we see a group of these diminutive bears having fun as they frolic through the countryside. One fairy rests among the sugar plums, while nearby a relaxing tune is played by the "Lily fairy." A large molehill provides a vantage point for the crescent moon bear to gaze down upon the young fairy practicing flight take-offs from the large toadstool, and another fairy steals a lift from a passing snail. This is all too much for the mother and her tiny baby, who appears rather bemused by all the hurrying and scurrying around them. Made of mohair and upholstery fabric, all the bears are fully articulated and soft-filled.

Index

Credits

The author would
like to thank the
artists who made
bears especially for
this book.

Also, Rosemary and
Paul Volpp, Joan
and Mike Woessner,
and my Mother,
who loaned some of
the artists' bears for
this book, and of
course all the other
artists I have
included for their
wonderful original
creations.

Dedication
To my Mother for
being the best Mum
in the world.